MW00439560

THOUGHTS OF
ST. IGNATIUS LOYOLA
FOR EVERY DAY OF THE YEAR

THOUGHTS OF
ST. IGNATIUS LOYOLA
FOR EVERY DAY OF THE YEAR

From the Scintillae Ignatianae
compiled by Gabriel Hevenesi, S.J.

Translated by Alan G. McDougall

Fordham University Press
New York

Adapted from Thoughts of St. Ignatius Loyola for Every Day in the Year, Translated from the "Scintillae Ignatianae" of Father Gabriel Hevenesi, S.J., by Alan G. McDougall (London: Burns Oates and Washbourne Ltd., 1928).

Library of Congress Cataloging-in-Publication Data

Ignatius, of Loyola, Saint, 1491-1556.
   Thoughts of St. Ignatius Loyola for every day of the year : from the Scintillae Ignatianae / compiled by Gabriel Hevenesi ; translated by Alan G. McDougall.—1st ed.
      p. cm.
   Includes bibliographical references.
   ISBN-13: 978-0-8232-2656-6
   ISBN-10: 0-8232-2656-5
   1. Devotional calendars—Catholic Church.   I. Hevenesi, Gabriel.
II. Title.
BX2170.C56I36 2006
242'.2—dc22

                                                2006024675

Printed in the United States of America
08   5 4
First edition

CONTENTS

Foreword to the 1928 Edition vii
   Alan G. McDougall

Introduction 1
   Patrick J. Ryan, S.J.

Thoughts of St. Ignatius Loyola
   for Every Day of the Year 14

FOREWORD TO THE 1928 EDITION

Scintillae Ignatianae, the compilation from which the following extracts are translated, was first published at Braunsberg in 1712. The author, a Hungarian Jesuit, was born at Miczke in 1656; entered the Society in 1671; became provincial of Austria, and died at Vienna in 1715. In the original collection each aphorism of St. Ignatius is followed by a short exposition by Fr. Hevenesi, in four clauses, meant to serve as the basis of a meditation. These expositions have been omitted in the present translation, and the saint left to speak for himself. In some half-dozen cases the translator, for various reasons, has ventured to substitute for the extract given by Fr. Hevenesi some other "thought" from the writings of St. Ignatius.

A.G.M.
In festo S Ignatii, 1928.

THOUGHTS OF
ST. IGNATIUS LOYOLA
FOR EVERY DAY OF THE YEAR

INTRODUCTION

Patrick J. Ryan, S.J.

At a precise date unknown to posterity, but probably sometime in the year 1491, there came to birth in the Basque area of northwestern Spain the last medieval man and the first modern man: Iñigo López de Loyola, better known today as Ignatius Loyola.

The first two names given to him at baptism link him to the medieval past. Iñigo, a pre-Roman Spanish name (Enneco in Latin), gave him as patron saint a Spanish Benedictine abbot of the eleventh century. In modern Basque the name is Eneko. López was a surname that derived from Lope, but by the late fifteenth century it had become a stock Spanish name. The "de Loyola" located this particular Iñigo López at the family estate and castle near Azpeitia that was the inheritance of his family, minor Basque nobility loyal to the court of Spain in the process of uniting that country under the Catholic rulers Ferdinand V of Aragon and Isabella I of Castille.[1]

The Basque country, never included in the Arab Muslim conquest of Spain in the eighth century, has remained to the present day a culturally distinct area, the Basque language having no links to Spanish or the other Romance or even Indo-European languages of western Europe. But the family of Iñigo had strong links to the Spanish monarchy and its crusade to win Spain back from Muslim dominance; the final act of that crusade, the conquest of Granada in 1492, took place the year after Iñigo's birth. The crusades, and especially the idealizing vision of crusaders and the knightly life characteristic of the popular romances of the day, gave a very medieval tinge to the imagination of Iñigo. In no place is this more obvious than in the analogy of an earthly king prefacing the Second Week of the *Spiritual Exercises*:

> I put before me a human king chosen by the hand of God Our Lord, to whom all Christian leaders and their followers give their homage and obedience. . . . [T]his king speaks to all his own saying: "My will is to conquer all the land of the infidels! Therefore all those who want to come with me will have to be content with the same food as I, the same drink, the same clothing, etc. Such persons will also have to work with me by day, and keep watch by night, etc., so that in this way they will afterwards share with me in the victory, as they have shared with me in the labours.". . . I consider what reply good subjects should make to such an open and kindly king, and on the other hand, if anyone refused to accept the request of such a king, how greatly such a person would deserve to be blamed by everyone and to be judged an unworthy knight. (*Spiritual Exercises*, no. 92)[2]

In his autobiographical memoir Iñigo mentions that the one literary diversion of his youth was "tales of chivalry,"[3] undoubtedly among them the best-seller of early sixteenth-century Spain, *Amadís de Gaula*. This lengthy potboiler, published in Spanish in 1508 by Garci Rodríguez de Montalvo, was based on much earlier sources (some of them Portuguese) purporting to tell the adventures of a knight from Wales (Gaula) in the era after King Arthur.

Fired with chivalric enthusiasm from reading such literature, Iñigo aspired to engage in bold knightly deeds of derring-do, apparently hoping thereby to win the notice and approval of a lady of the highest nobility, whose identity remains to the present day shrouded in mystery: "The lady was not of the ordinary nobility, nor a countess or a duchess: rather her state was higher than any of these."[4] One concrete knightly adventure undertaken by Iñigo involved his leading an outnumbered Spanish contingent in the defense of the fortress in Pamplona against French attackers on May 20, 1521. In the event, Iñigo sustained leg injuries that left him an invalid. Carried back to recuperate at length in the family keep at Loyola, Iñigo found to his disappointment that his pious sister-in-law kept no romances like *Amadís de Gaula* in the castle's meager collection of printed books. He had to settle instead for more religious fare: the fourteenth-century Ludolf of Saxony's *Life of Christ* and Jacobus de Voragine's *Golden Legend*, a thirteenth-century compilation of the lives of the saints.

Diverted from thoughts of fair ladies and knights in shining armor, the disabled Iñigo started to compare the inner reactions he used to have to the typical romances that had so enthralled him in times past with the new inner reactions he was having to the life of Christ and the lives of the saints. Although Iñigo used the medieval imagery of crusading chivalry to describe how the Christian should

3

respond to the call of Christ, he proved himself very modern and introspective in the attention he paid to his inner experiences:

> While reading the lives of Our Lord and the saints, he would stop to think, reasoning with himself: "How should it be, if I did this which St. Francis did, and this which St. Dominic did?" And thus he used to think over many things which he was finding good, always proposing to himself difficult and laborious things. And as he was proposing these, it seemed to him he was finding in himself an ease as regards putting them into practice. But his whole way of thinking was to say to himself: "St. Francis did this, so I must do it; St. Dominic did this, so I must do it."[5]

The "ease" Iñigo felt after reading the lives of St. Francis and St. Dominic was utterly different from how he felt when he reviewed in his mind the "tales of chivalry" he had once delighted in:

> The thoughts of the world mentioned above would follow, and on these too he would stop for a long while. . . . Still, there was this difference: that when he was thinking about that worldly stuff he would take much delight, but when he left it aside after getting tired, he would find himself dry and discontented.[6]

INTRODUCTION

Noticing the difference between the reflections that brought him ease and the thoughts that left him "dry and discontented" was the first step Iñigo took along the path of discernment of spirits. From his own experience of various spirits he began to understand the experiences of others, and this process led to the development of Iñigo as a spiritual director:

> I use the word "consolation" when any interior movement is produced in the soul that leads her to become inflamed with the love of her Creator and Lord, and when, as a consequence, there is no created thing on the face of the earth that we can love in itself, but we love it only in the Creator of all things. . . . "Desolation" is the name I give to everything contrary to [consolation] . . . , e.g., darkness and disturbance in the soul, attraction to what is low and of the earth, anxiety arising from various agitations and temptations. (*Spiritual Exercises*, nos. 316–17)[7]

Over the next two years Iñigo, guided by God's Spirit, pursued the calling he discerned in those experiences he had of consolation and desolation during his recuperation in the Loyola family castle. His experiences became even more intense when he took up the life of a mendicant and solitary in 1522 in and around Manresa in northeastern Spain. This mountainous village in Catalonia has, as a result, lent its name to numerous Jesuit retreat houses throughout the world. In 1523 Iñigo decided to go as a pilgrim to the Holy Land via Italy. Throughout these sometimes tortured years he gradually came to realize that he wanted to "help souls"[8] with similar experiences to find God's will in their lives. The book entitled *Spiritual Exercises* evolved as a handbook for those engaged in helping souls to discern where God was calling them; it was probably never meant to be handed to the one undergoing the controlled experience of discerning God's will. Perhaps that is the reason the *Spiritual Exercises* are not a literary masterpiece. Ignatius's aim in writing them was more pragmatic—to guide the director who was directing the "exercitant," the somewhat technical term used for one undergoing the exercises, emphasizing the personal activity it demands. They are quite frankly compared to physical exercises:

> For just as strolling, walking and running are exercises for the body, so "spiritual exercises" is the name given to every way of preparing and disposing one's soul to rid herself of all disordered attachments, so that rid of them one might seek and find the divine will in regard to the disposition of one's life for the good of the soul.[9]

The text of the *Spiritual Exercises* was only a manual; the actual exercises were to be the joint creation of God's Spirit and the human spirit, something so ineffable that no book could do them justice, although a director could serve as something of a referee or linesman for the one undergoing the experience of the *Spiritual*

Exercises, trying on behalf of the Church and the human community to prevent the exercitant from discerning his or her way to wild conclusions.

During the intense years Iñigo spent as a reflective invalid, penitential mendicant, pilgrim to Jerusalem, and solitary man of prayer, he gradually reached the conclusion that he could "help souls" better by becoming a priest. His hitherto limited education meant that he had to begin the study of Latin, the language of university education in sixteenth-century Europe; he was forced to do so with adolescents when he was already in his thirties.

Admitted to the University of Alcalà in 1526, he found the religious atmosphere fraught with suspicion of a relatively uneducated layman like himself sharing his religious experiences with his fellow students and even daring to direct them spiritually. A local version of the Inquisition closed in on him and he departed for the University of Salamanca, where he encountered the same religious suspicion. He later prefaced the text of the *Spiritual Exercises* with a plea for intellectual charity that is remarkably modern for a sixteenth-century Spanish Catholic, possibly a result of the lack of such charity he experienced in the universities of Spain:

> So that the director and the exercitant may collaborate better and with greater profit, it must be presupposed that any good Christian has to be more ready to justify than to condemn a neighbour's statement. If no justification can be found, one should ask the neighbour in what

7

sense it is to be taken, and if that sense is wrong he or she should be corrected lovingly. Should this not be sufficient, one should seek all suitable means to justify it by understanding it in a good sense. (*Spiritual Exercises*, no. 22)[10]

In the Latin translation of the *Exercises*, this paragraph is referred to as the *praesupponendum* and has entered into Jesuit vocabulary and spirituality as a central theme.

Iñigo left Spain for Paris at the beginning of 1528. There he began his humanistic studies all over again and eventually pursued philosophical and theological studies, free from excessive involvement in apostolic activities as well as the ecclesiastical restrictions that had been imposed on him in Spain and had kept him from sharing the experience of the *Spiritual Exercises* with others. It seems to have been at Paris, also, that he gradually changed his name to Ignatius, a tribute to the second-century martyr and bishop of Smyrna.

Over the next six years Ignatius gathered around him a group of student companions, all younger than he, including Francisco de Yasu y Xavier (Francis Xavier) and Pierre Favre (Peter Faber), with whom he shared the spiritual insights he had gained over the years since 1521. At the same time they shared with him not only their student apartment but also their greater academic abilities as they all prepared themselves for priestly ordination. On the Feast of the Assumption in 1534, at a Mass celebrated for them in a chapel on Montmartre by Faber, the first of the companions of Ignatius to be ordained a priest, Ignatius and his companions vowed themselves to a common missionary endeavor in the Holy Land. This project they only eventually abandoned, in 1537, when they found themselves at Venice and unable to travel to that area of the Middle East after war had broken out between the republic of Venice, allied with the papacy, and the Ottoman sultanate.[11] At that point Ignatius and his companions, all graduates of the University of Paris, pursued the alternative they already had in mind: to present themselves as a group to the currently reigning pope, the reformist Paul III, for whatever mission he would assign to them.

Another mark of the modernity of Ignatius can be found in the vision of the world beyond Europe that can be detected first of all in the text of the *Spiritual Exercises*. Immediately following the consideration on the Kingdom of Christ, replete as it is with recollections of the medieval knightly ideal, the exercitant is directed to look at the cosmos, from the viewpoint of the Trinity, in a contemplation on the Incarnation. But the cosmos viewed by the Trinity in the *Exercises* had expanded as seafaring explorers like Vasco da Gama and Christopher Columbus expanded the Iberian vision of the world:

> *Point I.* This is to see the various kinds of persons: first, those on the face of the earth, in all their diversity of dress and appearance, some white and some black, some in peace and others at war, some weeping and others laughing, some healthy, others sick, some being born and others dying. (*Spiritual Exercises*, no. 106)[12]

INTRODUCTION

Ignatius and his companions not only gave up on their plans to go to Jerusalem; they went instead to Rome to seek an apostolic mission from the pope. Thus they began the process by which they evolved from a devout company of educated clergymen recently ordained to becoming a new and very different religious order of men. Previously, such religious orders had been mainly monastic, or semimonastic, as in the congregations of friars. Stability of location, whole (as in the monastic orders) or partial (as in many congregations of friars), had significantly marked their foundations. Ignatius and his companions had a diametrically different vision of what the religious order they were founding would entail. Sent by the pope as head of the universal Church or by Ignatius standing in his place, the companions of Jesus, as they came to call themselves, dispersed almost immediately throughout Europe on various missions to reform a Church recognized as highly corrupt. Even more adventurously, at the invitation of King John III of Portugal, master of a far-flung Asian, African, and American empire then coming into existence, Francis Xavier set out to India via Portugal in 1540 and eventually to Indonesia and Japan, where he was the first Christian missionary, dying off the coast of China in 1552.

Ignatius kept in touch with his spiritual empire by detailed correspondence. In addition to elaborating the *Constitutions*, which were not quite complete at his death in 1556 and were accepted by the whole Society only two years later, he spent much of his time reading and responding to correspondence from his companions. The *Spiritual Exercises*, his partially complete autobiography as dictated to Luis Gonçalves da Câmara, his letters to all and sundry, and the *Constitutions* constitute the modest bibliography for the soldier who gradually became a spiritual leader of enormous magnitude.

About a century after the death of Ignatius on July 31, 1556, a child named Gabriel Hevenesi was born in what is now Hungary. Hevenesi entered the Society of Jesus in 1671 and occupied many positions of trust, including the office of provincial superior of the Jesuits in Austria. Three years before he died in 1715, Hevenesi put together a series of pithy sayings of Ignatius excerpted from his many writings but especially from his letters to various Jesuits. Hevenesi organized these quotations from Ignatius under the Latin title *Scintillae Ignatianae sive apophthegmata Sancti Ignatii per singulos anni dies distributae*—literally, "Ignatian sparks, or sayings, of Saint Ignatius distributed through every day of the year." The most recent Latin text of this work was published by the press of Friedrich Pustet in 1919 with 109 similar quotations from Saint Philip Neri appended to it. The last English edition of this work, minus Hevenesi's own meditations on these quotations from Ignatius and minus the abbreviated notices indicating whence the quotations derived, was translated and edited by Alan G. McDougall and published by the London-based press of Burns, Oates and Washbourne in 1928. McDougall admits at the beginning in his brief foreword that "in some half-dozen cases the translator, for various reasons, has ventured to substitute for the extracts given by Fr. Hevenesi some other 'thought' from the writings of St. Ignatius."[13]

In this year of triple jubilee for Jesuits, 2006—the four hundred fiftieth anniversary of the death of Ignatius and the five

INTRODUCTION

hundredth anniversaries of the births of Francis Xavier and Peter Faber—it seems only suitable that we return these pithy sayings of Ignatius to print. Even though they can too easily be read out of context, they can serve like the *Analects* of Confucius or the aphorisms of Charles de Montesquieu to summon up for us a whole man and a whole era very different from our own. And yet, for all their difference, the *Scintillae* of Ignatius still breathe with the unique personality, charming and yet challenging, of a man acutely aware of the age in which he lived and the challenges it posed to any faith-filled person. May these sparks once again ignite the fire of which Jesus himself spoke in words, in the Gospel of Luke, very much favored by Ignatius Loyola: "I have come to cast fire on the earth, and how I wish it were already blazing!" (Luke 12.49).

July 31, 2006

Four Hundred Fiftieth Anniversary
of the Death of Saint Ignatius Loyola
Fordham University
New York City

INTRODUCTION

NOTES

1. For the family origins of Ignatius, see Candido de Dalmases, S.J., *Ignatius of Loyola, Founder of the Jesuits*, trans. Jerome Aixala, S.J. (St. Louis: Institute of Jesuit Sources, in cooperation with Gujarat Sahitya Prakash, Anand, India, 1985), 3–27. Hereafter referred to as de Dalmases.

2. Saint Ignatius of Loyola, "The Spiritual Exercises" in *Personal Writings*, trans. Joseph A. Munitiz and Philip Endean (Harmondsworth: Penguin Books, 1996), 303. Hereafter, *PW.*

3. "Reminiscences (Autobiography)" in *PW*, 14.

4. *PW*, 15.

5. Ibid.

6. Ibid.

7. *PW*, 348–49.

8. On "helping souls," see *PW*, 24, and *The Constitutions of the Society of Jesus*, trans. George E. Ganss, S.J. (St. Louis: Institute of Jesuit Sources, 1970), 77–78.

9. *PW*, 283.

10. *PW*, 289.

11. de Dalmases, 148.

12. *PW*, 305.

13. Alan G. McDougall, foreword to *Thoughts of St Ignatius Loyola for Every Day in the Year,* trans. Alan G. McDougall (London: Burns Oates and Washbourne, 1928).

Vita beati P. Ignatii Loiolae Societatis Iesu fundatoris.
(The Life of St. Ignatius Loyola, Founder of the Society of Jesus)
Rome, 1609
Ignatius is severely wounded in the battle of Pamplona

January

1

All for the greater glory of God! St. Ignatius repeats these words and their like 376 times in his Constitutions.

2

Let your first rule of action be to trust in God as if success depended entirely on yourself and not on him: but use all your efforts as if God alone did everything, and yourself nothing.

3

The man who sets about making others better is wasting his time, unless he begins with himself.

4

Change of climate does not involve change of life. The imperfect man will be much the same wherever he is, until he has forsaken himself.

5

It is wrong to entrust difficult and dangerous affairs to the strength of young people.

6

One rare and exceptional deed is worth far more than a thousand commonplace ones.

7

You may be sure that the progress you make in spiritual things will be in proportion to the degree of your withdrawal from self-love and concern for your own welfare.

8

Nothing worthy of God can be done without earth being set in uproar and hell's legions roused.

9

You must strive much harder to tame the inner than the outer man, to break the spirit than the bones.

10

Great is the liberality of God: from him I obtain what I cannot get from men. Though they give me nothing, I shall gain all things from God.

11

It is God's habit of his goodness to defend most skillfully what the devil attacks most bitterly.

12

Charity and kindness unwedded to truth are not charity and kindness, but deceit and vanity.

13

The closer you bind yourself to God and the more wholeheartedly you give yourself up to his supreme majesty, the more liberal he will be to you.

14

The true religious is he who is wholly free not only from the world but from himself as well.

15

O God, if men only knew what thou art!

16

The evils of vanity and vainglory arise from ignorance and blind self-love.

17

To leave God for God's sake is no loss, but great profit, on the soul's balance sheet.

18

He who is zealous soars with wondrous speed in a few moments to a degree of virtue that the slothful cannot reach after many years.

19

Life would be unbearable to me if I found lurking in my soul anything human and not wholly divine.

20

We ought to consider not only God, but also men for his sake.

21

If it were possible for one who loved God to be damned without fault of his own, he could easily bear all the pains of hell save the blasphemies of the damned against God.

22

At times the devil torments a man so that he is, as it were, out of his mind: and hence it is that we sometimes put down to nature or sickness what ought to be ascribed to temptation.

23

Much more danger lurks in making light of little sins than of great ones.

24

Nothing resists the truth for long: it may be assailed, but never overcome.

25

When the devil wants to attack and harass a man with peculiar bitterness, he prefers to work at night.

26

To avoid disputes is a thing not only greathearted and worthy of the peace of the Christian spirit, but it is also justified by results.

27

It is dangerous to make everybody go forward by the same road: and worse to measure others by oneself.

28

All the good things God has created, weighed against prison, fetters, and disgrace, should count for nothing at all.

29

When everything goes as you want it to, put no trust in the continuance of your good fortune, but fear all the more.

30

In some matters silence is better than speech. When Truth is its own apologist, it needs no help from style.

31

If you are asked for anything you think it would be harmful to give, take care, though you refuse what is asked, to retain the asker's friendship.

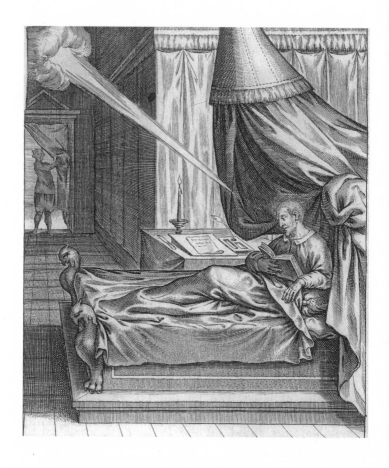

Vita beati P. Ignatii Loiolae Societatis Iesu fundatoris.
(The Life of St. Ignatius Loyola, Founder of the Society of Jesus)
Rome, 1609
*During his convalescence, Ignatius reads the life of Christ
and biographies of the saints*

February

1

He who is sick may safely refrain from the tasks of those in good health, and be content to make up for them by equanimity and patience, without ruining his body by toil.

2

If you want to be of use to others, begin by taking pains with yourself: the fire that is to enkindle others should be lighted at home.

3

In houses over which a calm and undisturbed tranquility is always brooding, it will go hard but some evils will make their nest.

4

It is a mistake to spend on prayer the efforts that ought to be directed to getting the affections under control.

5

Dwell not for a single night under the same roof with a man whose soul you know to be burdened with grievous sin.

6

So you lay your affairs aside till next month or next year? Why, where do you get your confidence that you will live so long?

7

When you undertake a contest, be sure always to have some support.

8

If you want to know what God requires of you, you must first of all put aside all affection and preference for one thing rather than another.

9

Never say or do anything until you have asked yourself whether it will be pleasing to God, good for yourself, and edifying to your neighbour.

10

He who wants to do great things in God's service must beware above all else not to be too clever.

11

Prudence belongs not to the one who obeys command, but to the one who gives it.

12

In a house that is well ordered the elders should live the life of the young, the younger the life of the mature, so that the former may display the keenness of youth, the latter the judgment of full age.

13

Better great prudence and ordinary holiness than great holiness and little prudence.

14

The laborers in the Lord's vineyard should have one foot on the ground, and the other raised to proceed on their journey.

15

He who has God lacks nothing, though he has nought else.

16

Even though they gave only equal, and not greater, glory to God, yet poverty, contempt, and a reputation for foolishness should be chosen with Christ rather than wealth, honor, and the repute of learning, since by choosing the former we more closely follow him.

17

When you say anything in secret, speak as if you were speaking to the whole world.

18

Religious who try to serve God in ways detrimental to their Rule pull down the tree in order to pluck the fruit.

19

If you want to bring anything to a successful conclusion, you must accommodate yourself to the task, not the task to yourself.

20

It is not enough that I should serve God by myself: I must help the hearts of all to love him and the tongues of all to praise him.

21

The devil never has greater success with us than when he works secretly and in the dark.

22

To have prevented one single sin is reward enough for the labors and efforts of a whole lifetime.

23

Ask God for grace to suffer much. To whom God gives this he gives a great gift: all his other benefits are included in this single one.

24

A healthy community must preserve itself and look to its welfare by cutting off its corrupt members in good time, before their rottenness reaches to the parts that are sound.

25

Better the forsaking of one's own will than the gift of raising the dead.

26

If signs are to be asked from God, the keeping of the precepts alone should require more and clearer signs than the keeping of the counsels.

27

A man who finds the path to virtue difficult, yet sets out on it bravely to conquer himself, gains double the reward of those whose mild and slothful nature gives them no trouble.

28

If you wish to live among and mix with your fellows securely, you must esteem it a matter of the first importance to be equally affected to all and partial to none.

29

If God makes you suffer greatly, it is a sign that he wants to make you a great saint.

Vita beati P. Ignatii Loiolae Societatis Iesu fundatoris.
(The Life of St. Ignatius Loyola, Founder of the Society of Jesus)
Rome, 1609
Ignatius offers his sword to the Madonna of Montserrat

March

1

God has much more regard for the interests of a man who puts himself and his own concerns in the second place and God's service first, than the man himself would have if he preferred his own business to God's.

2

He who seeks to scale the heights must go far down into the depths.

3

If a man wants to reform the world, either by reason of the authority of his position or the duty of his office, he must begin with himself.

4

If ever you find ignorant or malicious people calumniating you, pray God that the things they say may never be true.

5

I leave it to your good sense to decide which is better: to say now to all that is earthly, What does it profit a man? Or to cry in vain later on, What did it profit?

6

The man who has turned aside from the world should be like a statue, which refuses neither to be clothed with a rough garment nor to be despoiled of the rich robe it used to wear.

7

Less knowledge, more virtue!

8

All the honey of all the flowers in the world is not so sweet as the gall and vinegar of the Lord Jesus.

9

Even if I had all the money in the world, I would not give a penny to the man who by his own fault has become unworthy of the religious state.

10

Let it be your principle to allow others who are worldly-wise to begin the conversation, but keep the end for yourself, so that whatever be the metal of the speech, you may have a chance of transmuting it into gold.

11

It is but just that we should be deprived of divine consolation, seeing how lukewarm we are in spiritual things.

12

There is more to be learnt in one hour at Manresa with God for teacher than all the teachers in the world could impart.

13

There is no better wood for feeding the fire of God's love than the wood of the Cross.

14

I care but little for the fear of slavery or death that you put before me: the only fear that troubles me is the fear of offending God.

15

There is no storm worse than calm, and no foe more dangerous than to have no foes.

16

Nothing is sweeter than loving God—in such a way that you endure great things for his love.

17

The more desperate things seem, the more must we hope in God. When man's aid fails, God's is close at hand.

18

You will be helped more in procuring another man's salvation by meekness and humility than by authority; and you will gain your end sooner by yielding than by fighting.

19

Let one man's salvation be more to you than all the riches in the world.

20

A thing is worth just as much as God makes it worth.

21

I am glad when the good are well and the bad ill: so that the former may use all their strength for God's glory, and the latter may be led to him as they grow weaker.

22

If the guide God chooses for you to follow were only a little dog, you should not complain, but at God's command follow it willingly and gladly.

23

Never put off till tomorrow what you can do today.

24

It is far better to procure a mere morsel of some one good thing safely than to gain a hundred at the risk of your salvation.

25

We cannot expect too much from God, for with him it is as easy to perform as to will.

26

Give me only thy love and thy grace, O Lord, and I am rich enough; I ask for nothing more.

27

No created thing can give rise to any gladness in the soul that is worthy of comparison with the joy of the Holy Ghost.

MARCH

28
How earth stinks in my nostrils when I look up to heaven!

29
He who fears men much will never do anything great for God.

30
A rough and unshapen log has no idea that it can be made into a statue that will be considered a masterpiece, but the carver sees what can be done with it. So many seem to know scarcely anything of the Christian life and do not understand that God can mould them into saints, until they put themselves into the hands of that almighty Artisan.

31
The man who forgets himself and his own welfare for God's service will have God to look after him.

Vita beati P. Ignatii Loiolae Societatis Iesu fundatoris.
(The Life of St. Ignatius Loyola, Founder of the Society of Jesus)
Rome, 1609
In Manresa, Ignatius begins to write down his Spiritual Exercises

APRIL

1

Those who are elegant and foppish should be taught contempt of self and of every kind of preeminence in preference to and before bodily mortification.

2

In order that a man's natural gifts may be put to account for the salvation of souls, they must be set in motion by interior virtue, and strength obtained thereby for doing things well.

3

We should be slow to speak and patient in listening to all men, but especially to inferiors. Our ears should be wide open to our neighbor until he seems to have said all that is in his mind.

4

There is but one right kind of ambition: to love God, and as the reward of loving him, to love him more.

5

To gain men's goodwill in God's service we must become all things to all men; for men's hearts are gained by nothing so much as by similarity of habits and interests.

6

No one should call himself a friend of Christ unless he cherishes those souls that Christ redeemed by the shedding of his Blood.

7

Too frequent punishment is a sign of a rule that is impatient rather than desirous of discipline.

8

When people come to you in order to pass the time, talk to them of death, judgment, and other such grave matters. Thus their attention will be captured, even though they try to be deaf, and you will benefit both yourself and them. Either they will go away the better, or they will abstain from wasting your time in future.

9

I am at wondrous peace with the world so long as I do not make war on it, forgetting the tongue of my native land: but let me go forth to the camp, and you will see the whole city rise up against me while I fight on every side.

10

Do not look upon what you spend on natural needs as lost to religion.

11

The man who is going forth to labor in the Lord's vineyard should direct his steps by humility and self-contempt toward what is difficult and hard; for the rest of the building will be safely fixed if it is based on humility for its foundation.

12

We must not keep away from the Bread of Angels because we find no sensible delight therein: that would be like perishing of hunger because we had nothing tasty to eat.

13

He lives the blessed life who, so far as possible, has his mind continually fixed on God and God in his mind.

14

As we hold those dearer whom we find immovable in firmness of heart and manly virtue, so shall we more severely chastise their smallest faults.

15

Suffer nothing dirty or disordered about you. At the same time be careful to avoid that affected carefulness that savors of effeminacy and conceit.

16

Let the workman remember that his material is not gold, but clay, and let him keep a sharp eye on himself, lest he permit in himself a blemish such as he works hard to remove from others.

17

Beware of condemning any man's action. Consider your neighbor's intention, which is often honest and innocent, even though his act seems bad in outward appearance.

18

What is best in itself is not always most useful for everybody, but that should be done which in the actual circumstances is of most profit to each one.

19

However great your poverty, spare no expense that nothing may be wanting for the welfare of the sick.

20

He who knows God knows how to raise his mind immediately to God's love, not only when he beholds the starry heavens, but even on considering a blade of grass, or the smallest thing of any kind.

21

Love even the most abandoned: love whatever faith in Christ remains in them: if they have lost this, love their virtues; if these have gone, love the holy likeness they bear, love the blood of Christ through which you trust they are redeemed.

22

The man who professes to despise the world for Christ's sake has no country on earth to call his own.

23

Whatever you have to suffer that God may will, or that the devil with God's permission may bring upon you, nevertheless hope in God for victory.

24

I would not have the emotions, particularly anger, to be entirely extinguished and dead in those who are in authority, but kept in proper control.

25

Whatever suggestion comes to you from any source other than God or your rule is a temptation: hold it suspect.

26

To see a religious who seeks nothing but God sad, or one who seeks everything except God happy, is a great miracle.

27

It is the part of a reasonable man not only to curb his passions to prevent them from coming to light either in word or deed, but also to rule them in such a way that everything is done by reason, nothing on impulse.

28

Take care lest the children of this world spend more care and attention on transitory things than you do on seeking those that are eternal.

29

A little thing well grounded and lasting is better than a great thing that is uncertain and insecure.

30

Whatever is done without the will and consent of the director is to be imputed to vainglory, not merit.

Vita beati P. Ignatii Loiolae Societatis Iesu fundatoris.
(The Life of St. Ignatius Loyola, Founder of the Society of Jesus)
Rome, 1609
On the Mount of Olives, Ignatius prays before the footprints of Christ

MAY

1

In judging of what you are to choose, you should consider not the plausibility of appearances, but look forward to the end.

2

God leads us by a twofold way: one, unknown because hidden, is taught by himself; the other he allows to be shown us by men.

3

It is better to go on living without the certainty of blessedness, and serve God and seek your neighbor's salvation the while, than to die at once with the assurance of glory.

4

A man may be justified in using less care about human concerns; but to serve the immortal God negligently is in no wise to be borne.

5

God is no blind moneychanger; he values love's works more than its words.

6

There are three sure marks of the good state of a religious house: the observance of the enclosure, of purity, and of silence.

7

Against that vice you should lay hold of those arms to which you feel most moved, and not sound the retreat until, by God's guidance, you have conquered it.

8

A man who is secretly depraved and lives among those who delight in uprightness will not remain with them for long.

9

A man who is subject to motions of anger should not withdraw from the company of others: for such movements are overcome, not by flight, but by resistance.

MAY

10

We should avoid excessive dealings with women, even those who are religious: for there always arises from it either smoke or fire.

11

In helping our neighbor we should be like the angels, who neglect no kind of toil in their care for men's salvation, yet lose none of their blessed and everlasting peace, whatever their success.

12

I would rather have God's servants remarkable for virtue than for numbers, and manifest rather by the reality of their service than their repute for it.

13

Let us go forth eagerly, sure that whatever cross we have to bear will not be without Christ, and that his aid, more powerful than all the plots of our enemies, will always be with us.

14

Let your garb, as is fitting, be decent, in accordance with local custom, and suitable to your condition and profession.

15

If the devil urges you to sin by an unwonted onslaught of evil thoughts, you must have recourse also to unwonted remedies for the sudden attack as well as to the usual ones.

16

Let superiors take care not to estrange their subjects by asperity; a mere suspicion of severity is harmful.

17

He who is going to enter religion must know that he will not find continual calm and rest therein unless he cross the threshold with both feet, the will and the judgment, at once.

18

Spend whatever is necessary on the care of the sick; we who are well can easily manage with dry bread, if there is nothing else.

MAY

19

You should trust in God enough to believe that you could cross the seas on a bare plank if there were no ship.

20

When a superior commands you to do anything, you may still use prudence in doing it.

21

It would indeed be a great miracle if God left destitute of his help those who for the sake of his love have given up the power to help themselves.

22

Let he who is rich strive to possess his goods, not be possessed by them.

23

Success and dryness are equally dangerous to those who are given to prayer: the one tends to make the mind swell with pride, the other provokes it to boredom.

24

We are not masters of our body, but God; and so its mortifications cannot be meted out with the same measure to everyone.

25

It is the devil's habit to do his business out of doors rather than at home. God, on the other hand, works at man and moves him inwardly rather than outwardly.

26

When the devil wants to attack anyone, he first of all looks to see on what side his defenses are weakest or in worst order; then he moves up his artillery to make a breach at that spot.

27

I beseech you in the grace of Jesus Christ, forget those things that are behind, and as if you had just begun your long journey for the first time, set out eagerly on the way of virtue with unwearied step.

28

It is certain that the lazy will never come to peace of mind or the perfect possession of virtue, since they do not conquer themselves; while the diligent easily obtain both in a few days.

29

If a soldier in time of war fights better to gain worthless glory and spoil than you, who from the victory you strenuously obtain are to gain eternal glory in the kingdom of heaven, you are soldiers of Christ neither in name nor in fact.

30

The most precious crown is reserved in heaven for those who do all that they do as zealously as possible: for to do good deeds in not enough by itself; we must do them well.

31

I would have every one of you above all things to be glowing with a pure and sincere love of Jesus Christ our Savior, and with a zeal for God's glory and your neighbor's salvation.

Vita beati P. Ignatii Loiolae Societatis Iesu fundatoris.
(The Life of St. Ignatius Loyola, Founder of the Society of Jesus)
Rome, 1609
In Paris, Ignatius wins new companions

JUNE

1

Strive after the end to which you are called with all your might, since God has supplied you with so many aids and means thereto.

2

How few there are who use for their salvation the gift of Jesus' Blood!

3

Not only ought you to continually love and cherish each other but to communicate that love to all men.

4

How few people realize what God would do for them if they were to give themselves up wholly into his hands!

5

They who, though they indeed do what their superiors order, yet do it unwillingly and without interior consent, are to be numbered with the vilest slaves.

6

As we have made a bad use of the powers of our body and mind in acting against God's law, so, now that by penance we have been restored to grace, let us use the same powers to amend our lives.

7

The wise fisher of men, in order to gain all, ought to attune himself to all, even though his attempts have small success.

8

When everything goes favorably, beware lest all is not so well as it might be with the service of God.

9

A system of mortification openly pursued, over and above that which one's rule prescribes, is rightly prohibited; both that we may be mindful that obedience is better than sacrifice, and that we may not extol ourselves foolishly.

JUNE

10

We must use the same weapons against the devil for our salvation as he abuses for our destruction.

11

Those who in the world would, through nature's bounty, have met with the best fortune have likewise greater success in zealously showing forth the glory of God.

12

When storms rage against us through no fault of our own, it is a kind of pledge of success in the near future.

13

Persecution is the bellows that fans the flame of our virtue: if it were lacking—which God forbid—our strength would die away and not perform its task rightly.

14

Lord, what do I want, what can I want, apart from thee?

15

Those who obey with the will alone, while their reason is still unsubdued, walk lamely in the religious life.

16

Behold, with heartfelt and deep sorrow, in what great ignorance of God everyone remains!

17

We must strive as hard as we can to lay hold of that we follow after, and having entered the way of perfection, attain to what is most perfect.

18

There is no wild beast on earth fiercer, keener, or more persistent in injuring man than the devil, that he may fulfill the desire of his malicious and obstinate mind for our destruction.

19

You cannot speak of the things of God to any man, even the worst, without his gaining much profit thereby.

JUNE

20

Never tickle a man's ears with promises too great for your actions to correspond with them.

21

To hate the shortcomings of others too keenly is productive of estrangement rather than amendment, and serves to put people to flight rather than to help them.

22

The best kind of mortifications are those that, while their sting is sharper, do less hurt: for by these the body is afflicted both more annoyingly and more lastingly.

23

Do nothing and write nothing that may be the occasion of any bitterness or harsh words.

24

The devil has much joy of a soul that works indiscreetly, without being held in check by him who ought to rule it: for the higher such a one strives to mount, the greater its fall.

25

Speak little, listen much.

26

He who carries God in his heart bears heaven with him wherever he goes.

27

The shortest—almost the only—path to salvation is to turn resolutely away from everything that the world loves and cleaves to.

28

It is a mistake to measure a man's progress by his look, his gestures, his good nature, or his love of solitude, when it ought to be estimated from the violence he does himself.

29

The more useful the conversation of one who is fervent with outsiders is if it be good, the more harmful is it if it be dissolute.

June

30

It is a great help to progress to possess a friend who is privileged to point out to you your failings.

Vita beati P. Ignatii Loiolae Societatis Iesu fundatoris.
(The Life of St. Ignatius Loyola, Founder of the Society of Jesus)
Rome, 1609
Ignatius and his companions make their vows in Montmartre

July

1

It is part of a good religious to urge men to the service not of their prince but of God, that he may show that in choosing such a Lord he has done the best thing possible.

2

The good hunter of souls ought to conceal many things as if he did not know them; afterward, when he is master of the will, he can bend the novice in virtue whither he lists.

3

How greatly mistaken are those who, while thinking themselves to be full of the spirit, are eager for the government of souls!

4

To seek to bring all men to salvation by one road is very dangerous. He who does so fails to understand how many and various are the gifts of the Holy Ghost.

5

Nothing makes religious more contemptible in the world's eyes than to see them divided into parties and sects among themselves.

6

To do many things and to mix with many people, yet not to turn aside from either God or oneself, is a great and rare art.

7

Virtue and holiness of life can do a great deal, almost everything, with men, as well as with God.

8

Check impulse with impulse, habit with habit, as one nail is blunted with another.

9

It is stupid to neglect an immediate opportunity of serving God in the hope of doing something greater in future: for it may well be that you will lose the one without gaining the other.

10

When the devil instills into your mind mean and petty thoughts, turn your memory to the benefits God has shown you in times past.

11

When the devil cannot bring you to commit sin, he will take a delight in annoying you and filching your peace of mind.

12

It is God's habit to put just so much value on anything as that thing is joined to him as an instrument for doing good.

13

The man of prayer must not be cast down in aridity, nor elated when he receives consolation. In dryness let him remember the graces he has enjoyed; and when he feels sensible devotion, let him consider it an alms given him gratis by God.

14

Workers for the salvation of souls ought so to labor as to make themselves acceptable not only to God but also to men for his sake; and regulate their zeal for the divine honor by their neighbor's progress.

15

Act toward the wicked like the loving mother who is tormented with pity for her sick child, and caresses him with no less ardor when he is ill than when he is strong and well.

16

So that our self-love may not lead us astray in dealing with matters that concern ourselves, we should think of them as if they concerned others, that thus our judgment may be guided by truth and not by affection.

17

We do not learn so much from conversation or argument as from humble recourse to God.

18

Your cowardice makes the devil bolder, just as women are bold only when they see that their lovers are soft.

19

For correction to be of any use, either he who corrects must have authority, or he who is corrected proved love.

20

If a man is not moved to forsake all that is his for God, let him nonetheless refer all things to him; many though they be, they will always be less than that one thing that Christ called needful.

21

Whether the body be made prone to some fault by softness, or weakened by excessive severity, an account must equally be rendered to God—even though the latter course may seem to have been undertaken for his honor and glory.

22

The sharper you are at noticing other people's failings, the more apt will you be to overlook your own.

23

Many folk are drawn to love virtue more through its being commended by a man they esteem than for its own sake.

24

Children may be brought to virtuous ways and actions by presents and sweetmeats, as a pet animal by those who smile at it.

25

Better to get what you want by a request or a gift than by fighting for it.

26

You must attend to both kinds of mortification, interior and exterior; but with this difference, that the former is the principal, to be sought always and by everyone, the latter is to be measured by the circumstances of place, person, and time.

27

A fault that might easily be overcome at its first appearance becomes unconquerable through passing of time and habitual giving way.

28

Let us think of nothing but serving God: he will readily provide whatever else we need.

29

A man who has control over the motions of his heart gains more by a quarter of an hour's meditation than another does in many hours.

30

The sayings of backbiters are to be refuted by the testimonies of good men; and the mouth of him that speaks iniquity stopped by good deeds.

31

Nothing more desirable or gladsome can happen than to die for Christ's sake and our neighbor's salvation.

Vita beati P. Ignatii Loiolae Societatis Iesu fundatoris.
(The Life of St. Ignatius Loyola, Founder of the Society of Jesus)
Rome, 1609
In Venice, Ignatius, with his companions, is ordained a priest

AUGUST

1

In your good works and holy exercises, avoid all sloth and lukewarmness as your worst enemy.

2

Those who are specially remarkable for birth, learning, or wit ought to give themselves up more than ever to self-abnegation, or they will come to greater harm than the humble and unlearned.

3

To prevent us doing a good deed, the devil often suggests to us a better: then he raises fresh difficulties and obstacles to prevent our doing that.

4

A superior ought to treat his subjects in such a way that they may be cheerful, free from sadness, and serve God with a serene mind.

5

When taking the first steps on the road of virtue the old man must be mortified, but in such a way as not to slay the new man.

6

In particular, do not embark on affairs of public interest, which will be open to the observation and criticism of the many, unless you foresee a way of bringing them to a successful conclusion.

7

When, as is but human, errors are committed by others, you should see in them, as in a mirror, some deformity that needs removing in yourself.

8

If you begin by winning your own approval, you will easily command that of others.

9

Do everything you do without expecting praise: but let everything you do be such as cannot justly be blamed.

10

Know a man thoroughly before becoming his friend.

11

How much a man loses, not only of liberty but of authority, who accepts gifts!

12

Make no decision about anything when the mind is biased either by affection or by great dejection. Put it off till the anxiety has disappeared, so that you may do what mature reason, not impulse, dictates.

13

So order the inner man that its order overflows into the outer.

14

He who goes about to reform the world must begin with himself, or he loses his labor.

15

If your neighbor's sin is so manifest that you cannot in honesty excuse it, blame not the sinner but the violence of his temptation, remembering that you yourself might have fallen as badly or even worse.

16

In the matter of your neighbor's salvation authority is necessary, but not the kind that partakes of the vain authority of the world.

17

Avoid all obstinacy; but when you have begun a thing well, stick to it, and do not basely flee through weariness or despair.

18

Serving the world halfheartedly matters little; but serving God halfheartedly is not to be borne.

19

Rare indeed is the man who knows all his weaknesses of all kinds, unless God specially reveals them to him.

20

Those who have care of souls need nothing so much as courage, lest, while they are looking after others' salvation, they endanger their own.

21

"I will" and "I will not" are strangers in this house.

22

If the body complains of being mortified on the pretext that it is ill, it is not to be listened to in the hope of ease, but chastised by the substitution of some other equal mortification.

23

It is best to converse with seculars of matters relating to salvation in the morning, and of profane matters after midday.

24

Nothing that is not in itself evil is to be put away because abuse of it is possible: to do so would shut the way to a great increase of God's glory.

25

A little holiness and great health of body does more in the care of souls than great holiness and little health.

26

Has God put you into this world so that you may live as if there were no such things as heaven and hell? Is getting saved so easy a business that you need not trouble yourself about it?

27

If we were to die now, what would happen to us? What account should we give of the many riches, graces, and companions left to perish through our means?

28

At one moment the devil takes away all fear, lest you fall: at another he increases it, that you may yield: and both to your destruction.

29

Never contradict anybody, with cause or without; but always accept what others approve.

30

What is poisonous in books spreads far, unless it is opposed at the beginning.

31

It is not fitting that those who are implicated in their own affairs should immediately turn to the things of the soul: that would be like casting a hook without worm or bait.

Vita beati P. Ignatii Loiolae Societatis Iesu fundatoris.
(The Life of St. Ignatius Loyola, Founder of the Society of Jesus)
Rome, 1609
*At La Storta, outside Rome, Ignatius has a vision
of God the Father and of Christ*

September

1

Men of great virtue, though their learning for their neighbors' help be small, preach more eloquently and persuade their people to goodness more powerfully by their appearance than they could by rhetorical skill, however highly instructed they were.

2

If the pricks of a still partly untamed nature call forth from us words or deeds unsuited to our profession, so we must repress them all the more severely when they are obedient to us.

3

Desire to be openly known to everyone, both inwardly and outwardly.

4

Do not be familiar with or at the beck and call of everyone, but consult the Spirit as to whom he most urges you.

5

Seek to be held a fool by all men, that God may account you wise.

6

The best kind of obedience is that which in its eagerness to obey does not wait either for the necessity of the highest command or the intimation of an order.

7

A superior ought to root out errors immediately, lest, if he wink at them once or twice, custom become law.

8

Conquer yourself; for if you do this you will gain a brighter crown in heaven than others who are meeker by nature.

9

Do not use asperity toward those of little strength, lest the degree of evil that may arise with its consequent despair be much greater than the good to be expected from a severe rebuke.

10

Against the devil's daily wiles it is fitting to keep daily watch at stated times, and to enter diligently into oneself, so as to consider all our words, deeds, and thoughts in the presence of God.

11

If you promise anything for tomorrow, do it today rather than put it off.

12

If a man publicly reviles princes or magistrates, he rather gives rise to harm and scandal than offers a remedy.

13

To foresee what we shall have to do, and to call up for judgment what we have done, are the most trustworthy rules for right action.

14

If you find you have fallen, do not despair; even falls are an aid to well-being.

15

Do not put off the mortification of your body or your passions till old age, which is uncertain and cannot endure hardness.

16

Though all men and all reasons persuade us thereto, we should begin no business till we have first consulted God in prayer.

17

Meditation and converse with God constrains the power of free nature and checks its impulses.

18

If you want to make progress in love, speak about love; for holy conversation, like a breeze, fans the flame of charity.

19

Nothing is hard to a man whose will is set on it, especially if it be a thing to be done out of love.

20

To one who possesses God nothing troublesome can happen; for God cannot be lost, unless we will to lose him; and all sadness arises from our losing, or fearing to lose, some good thing.

21

When I am serving those who are servants of my Lord, I consider that I am doing the service of my Lord himself.

22

God would readily give us much greater graces if our perverse wills did not stand in the way of his bounty.

23

All of us are bound by a common obligation to rejoice in the good and profit of God's image, which he redeemed with the precious Blood of his only begotten Son.

24

So that our handling of great affairs may go as we wish, the smallest concerns are to be sent before them, that so we may ask for the great ones the help of him who gives grace to the humble.

25

God's supreme goodness, mighty love, and fatherly care are more ready freely to bestow perfection on us than we are to seek it out.

26

The evils of the soul arise from excess, whether of lukewarmness or of fervor.

27

Rare indeed are good workmen of the kind that seek not their own things, but the things of Jesus Christ.

28

It often happens that others' works are impeded for our sake, when we ought to manifest our own to others.

29

The fall of one man is a terror to others, and casts a damper on the fervor of many in the way of virtue.

30

In my heart I hear a music that has no words, a harmony that has no sound: yet so gladsome is what I hear that nothing in the world can be compared thereto.

Vita beati P. Ignatii Loiolae Societatis Iesu fundatoris.
(The Life of St. Ignatius Loyola, Founder of the Society of Jesus)
Rome, 1609
Ignatius receives from Pope Paul III papal approval of the Order

OCTOBER

1

If discretion seem to you a rare thing and hard to obtain, supply the lack of it by obedience: have recourse to that, and you will be safe.

2

When an untamed and intractable horse is piled up with many burdens beyond his strength, spurs are applied to him, not the bridle.

3

You do a great deal by the mere intention of undertaking labor for souls.

4

A good life is much better than learning, whether for obtaining or for communicating to others the gifts of the Holy Ghost.

5

The concern of serving our neighbor, which extends far and wide on all sides, is gathered up together in holy desires and prayers.

6

Go and set the whole world on fire.

7

One who is bound by so great an obligation to serve God as you are must not be content with ordinary labor and service.

8

How great a risk salvation and innocence run amid those storms and tempests that are roused at one moment by the raging whirlwind of goods and wealth, at another by honor and glory, at another by pleasure!

9

We may fairly hope that together with our spiritual good our earthly good also will not fail to increase.

10

God has chosen you out lest miserable and transitory human concerns should keep your mind ensnared and your heart distracted this way and that.

11

As cleanliness that is modest and sober is the token of a composed and ordered mind, so if it is excessive—and this usually arises from eagerness to please—it is to be accounted as neglect.

12

The man who gazes on heaven with a clear eye will see all the better the darkness of earthly things: for though these emit a certain kind of brilliance, the splendor of heaven darkens all their light.

13

The difference between a pious man and a vain one is that the one abstains from earthly things and abounds in spiritual consolations: the other delights in sensuous things and is tormented by interior ones.

14

The evil man is ready to suspect others, like a man attacked by giddiness who thinks that all things are whirling round him, not from any fault of theirs, but because of the disturbed humors of his own head.

15

A member that is torn away from the body receives therefrom neither motion nor feeling, nor any life at all.

16

The difference between human felicity and the cross of Christ is this, that on tasting the former we loathe it, but the more we drink of the latter, the greater is our thirst.

17

We ought always to hold in suspicion the accusations our body makes against us, for it is accustomed to plead a pretended lack of strength to disguise a yearning to escape hardship.

18

Self-love does a great deal; frequently it deludes our mind's eye so as to make us think things impossible that, if we saw them clearly, would evidently appear easy and even necessary.

19

The fullness of God's consolation is so great that the sweetness of it not only touches the soul, but even overflows to the body.

20

Since the object of our love is infinite, we can always love more and more perfectly.

21

The lover of voluntary poverty should be like a statue, enduring rags or fine linen and purple with unchanged countenance.

22

When you render assistance to virtue, you are at the same time having regard to your neighbor's salvation.

23

To the just man even the strokes of adverse fortune are of profit: while hurting they advantage him, like a dew of precious stones depriving the vine of its leaves to bestow on it a better treasure.

24

O God of supreme goodness, how canst thou endure so foul a sinner as I?

25

He who loves perfection must be filled with humility like a lamp with oil: for lamps are full within and give light without, and their influence makes itself felt in whatever direction they are turned.

26

Whatever graces from God you find in yourself, look upon as gold and gems that the goodness of God the goldsmith has mercifully created out of wood fit only for the fire.

27

Better to die a violent death than to live for vanity.

28

Though by nature alone the assent of the judgment is moved toward what offers the appearance of truth, yet in many things, those namely wherein the evidence of known truth offers no support, it can be bent by the weight of the will to one side rather than the other.

29

If you seek peace and tranquillity, you will certainly not find them so long as you have a cause of disturbance and turmoil within yourself.

30

God's liberality will supply in abundance from its own store the gain that he sees you despise for his sake.

31

If you do not lack humility and meekness, so neither will you lack God's goodness to aid you.

Vita beati P. Ignatii Loiolae Societatis Iesu fundatoris.
(The Life of St. Ignatius Loyola, Founder of the Society of Jesus)
Rome, 1609
Ignatius sends Francis Xavier to India as a missionary

NOVEMBER

I

The soul's desire is satisfied not by abundance of knowledge, but by an inward feeling and taste for things.

2

Without temperance and moderation, good degenerates into evil and virtue into vice.

3

The devil often acts in such a way as to curtail the time set apart for meditation or prayer.

4

The more a man withdraws himself from all his friends and acquaintances and from care for all things human, the more progress he will make in the spiritual life.

5

There ought to be no questioning whether one's superior is good or middling or poor: such a distinction takes away the virtue of obedience.

6

The closer we draw to God, the better disposed we are to receive the gifts of his divine bounty.

7

Every Christian ought in love to prefer rather to turn to good another's doubtful opinion or proposal than to condemn it.

8

As often as we manifest others' failings we show up our own.

9

But if anyone has without sufficient consideration chosen a course from which he may lawfully withdraw, it remains that when he begins to repent of doing so, he should make up for his wrong choice by good life and zealous deeds.

10

Let your modesty be a sufficient incitement, yea, an exhortation to everyone to be at peace on their merely looking at you.

November

11

He who is making a choice ought to examine himself whether the affection that he has towards anything arises solely from love of God and regard to him.

12

It is the part of God and of every good angel to infuse true spiritual joy into the soul.

13

Often, especially when one has but lately embarked on a better life, a scruple is of no little help to the mind empty of spiritual things.

14

Just as it is harmful to defame superiors in public, so it is worthwhile to admonish in private those who, if they would, could amend evils.

15

The Catholic Church is but one; for as the Bridegroom is one, the Bride must be one also. Between the Bridegroom and the Bride there is one and the same spirit.

16

The more exactly a superior knows the whole inner life of his subjects, the more is he able to assist them with greater diligence, love, and care.

17

The grace of speech in conducting necessary business with one's neighbor is greatly to be desired.

18

All contempt of earthly things will be helpful to union on both sides, for in these self-love, the most dangerous enemy of this union and universal good, is wont to wander.

19

When you are tempted, summon to your assistance the hope and thought that consolation will shortly follow, especially if by holy struggles you gradually overcome the struggles of despair.

20

Let the capable ruler beware lest some particular affection endanger his general charity.

21

It is hard to tarry on earth, unless your conversation be rather in heaven and in God through charity than on earth and with yourself: like the sun's rays, which shine forth from the sun and endure, so long as their life is in the sun.

22

When despair shows itself, man is driven by the evil spirit, at whose instigation nothing is ever done well.

23

It is the part of a truly prudent man to put no trust in his own prudence, especially in regard to his own concerns, of which a man whose mind is disturbed can hardly be a good judge.

24

A religious ought to be more afraid of the fear of poverty than of poverty itself.

25

The more you converse with and make friends of spiritual men, the greater will be your delight in God.

26

The providence of our most loving Father and wise Physician purges all the more in this world those whom he most loves, and whom he wishes most speedily to bring after this life to eternal happiness.

27

It should constantly be our care to see God's presence in everything, and not only to raise our minds to him when we are at prayer.

28

Above all we must consider what God will require of us in his judgment, what explanation of our actions he will demand, so that we may arrange our lives to accord with his judgment and not with our own inclination.

November

29

The way to avoid distress and affliction of mind in this world is to strive to conform our will wholly to God's.

30

Experience shows that the most frequent contradictions are followed by the greatest fruit.

Vita beati P. Ignatii Loiolae Societatis Iesu fundatoris.
(The Life of St. Ignatius Loyola, Founder of the Society of Jesus)
Rome, 1609
Death of Ignatius

December

1

When the devil meets with a too delicate conscience, he tries to make it much more delicate, and to reduce it to extreme distress, so that it may be so wretchedly disturbed as at last to fall out of the race for spiritual improvement.

2

Use and experience teach that it is not the lazy and listless, but the ardent and eager, who enjoy calm and peace of mind in God's service.

3

Almost the whole life of religious bodies lies in the maintenance of their first fervor.

4

The more detached and solitary a soul becomes, the better fitted it grows to seek and find its Creator.

5

Great is the error of those who, blinded by self-love, think that they are being obedient when by some argument they bring their superior to agree to what they themselves want.

6

A soul that desires to make progress in the spiritual life must go in the opposite direction from the devil's leading.

7

Give me humility, O Lord, but of such a kind that it permits of and includes the love of thee.

8

Mary grieves more at her Son's being offended by men's sins than she did for his crucifixion.

9

You owe obedience to your superior not on account of his prudence or goodness or any other gifts of God he may possess, but solely because he stands in God's place in regard to you.

10

Let everyone set before himself for his imitation those whom he sees to be noteworthy for zeal and greatness of spirit.

11

To subdue the spirit is harder than to afflict the flesh.

12

Negligence and lukewarmness always make labor a sad business for the slothful.

13

We may be quite sure that God is always ready to be liberal, provided he find in us a deep and true humility.

14

Many things, often even good ones, can be left undone, and things done that, though they do not amount to sins, ought not to be done, for the sake of men whom we desire to profit.

15

Listening is easier than speech.

16

A judge does ill to believe an accuser, unless on hearing the accused he finds him guilty.

17

Undertake nothing without consulting God.

18

Truth always shines with its own light, while a lie is hidden in darkness: but the mere presence of the reality is enough to dispel that darkness.

19

Attend as much as you can to this, that you regard one another kindly, so that there may be natural love between you.

DECEMBER

20

When kindness toward a man turns out useless, severity will be useful as an example to others.

21

No man is to be offended, least of all those who, if they were our enemies, might impede our progress in God's service and in zeal for the general welfare.

22

Penitence should include contrition of heart, confession of the lips, and satisfaction in act.

23

The Holy Ghost, who moves you to make your choice, will easily supply the manner and form of the choice.

24

An innocent and holy life, it is true, in itself counts for much, and is to be preferred far above all else; but unless it be combined with prudence in your relations with other men, it will be weak and insecure.

25

Count yourselves but worthless, mean-spirited, cowardly, and slothful if there be one man found at court who, to gain an earthly king's favor, obeys his commands more faithfully than you do those of the King of heaven, in order that you may be found pleasing in his sight.

26

Everything you say and do will come to light: remember that what you say in secret will be shouted from the housetops.

27

Those who are too cautious in matters relating to God seldom do anything great and heroic; a man who is terrified of every little difficulty that may occur does not undertake such things.

28

When an affair has been discussed and decided, do not act until you have slept on it.

29

As far as possible give no foothold to sloth, the source of all evils.

30

As one who strives to cast out an evil thought gains a great reward in heaven, so he who does not consent to good inspirations runs a grave risk of falling into great evils.

31

Praise and thanksgiving to God our Creator, from whose infinite liberality and bounty overflows the fullness and fruit of all good things.

À LA CROISÉE DES MONDES / 3
LE MIROIR D'AMBRE

n° 1205

Lyra est retenue prisonnière par Mme Coulter, qui, pour mieux s'assurer de sa docilité, l'a plongée dans un sommeil artificiel. Will, le compagnon de Lyra, armé du poignard subtil, s'est lancé à sa recherche, escorté de deux anges. Il délivre son amie mais, à son réveil, Lyra lui annonce qu'une mission encore plus périlleuse les attend: ils doivent descendre dans le monde des morts.

Le papier de cet ouvrage est composé de fibres naturelles,
renouvelables, recyclables et fabriquées à partir de bois
provenant de forêts gérées durablement.

Photocomposition : CPI Firmin-Didot

Loi n° 49-956 du 16 juillet 1949
sur les publications destinées à la jeunesse
ISBN : 978-2-07-509123-7
Numéro d'édition : 362761
Premier dépôt légal dans la collection : octobre 2017
Dépôt légal : septembre 2019

Imprimé en Espagne par Novoprint (Barcelone)